Audio Access Included - *Recorded Accompaniments Online*

AMERICAN ART SONGS
FOR THE PROGRESSING
TENOR

ISBN 978-1-4950-8855-1

To access companion recorded piano accompaniments online, visit:
www.halleonard.com/mylibrary

Enter Code
6604-3534-0641-6479

G. SCHIRMER, *Inc.*

DISTRIBUTED BY

HAL•LEONARD®

7777 W. BLUEMOUND RD. P.O. BOX 13819 MILWAUKEE, WI 53213

www.musicsalesclassical.com
www.halleonard.com

Pianists on the recordings: [1]Brendan Fox, [2]Laura Ward

SHENANDOAH

American Sea Chanty
Arranged by Celius Dougherty

Fare - well, my dear - est, __ I'm bound to leave you; Hi - o! you roll-ing

riv - er, O Shen - an - do - ah, __ I'll not de - ceive you, Hi - o! I'm bound a -

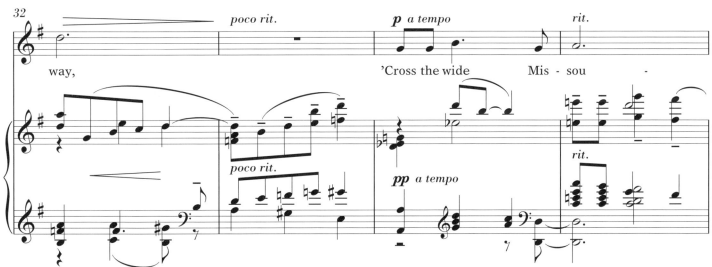

poco rit.   p a tempo   rit.

way,   'Cross the wide   Mis - sou -

a tempo

ri. _____

HEY NONNY NO!

Anonymous (16th century)

Samuel Barber

With boisterous good-humor!

Hey non-ny no! Hey non-ny no! Men are fools that wish to
die! _____

Is't not fine to dance and sing _____ When the bells of death do ring?

There are no dynamics in Barber's manuscript; minimal suggestions have been made.

Is't not fine to swim in wine, ___ And turn up-on the toe, ___

And sing ___ hey non-ny no! When the winds blow and the seas flow?

faster

Hey non-ny no! ___ Hey non-ny no! Hey non-ny no!

slower   *a tempo*

[*cresc.*]   [*f*]

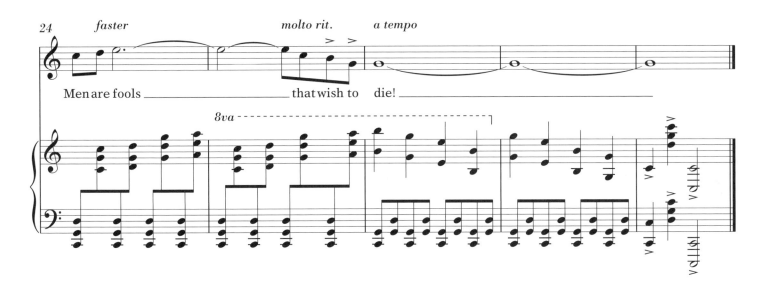

Men are fools ___ that wish to die! ___

faster   *molto rit.*   *a tempo*

8va -

To Daisy
THE DAISIES
from *Three Songs*

James Stephens

Samuel Barber
Op. 2, No. 1

In the scent-ed bud   of the morn ing—O,   When the wind - y grass went rip - pling   far,   I saw my   dear one walk - ing slow   In the field   where the dais - ies   are.   We did not laugh,   and we did not speak,   As we

The lyrics in the music read:

wan-dered hap-p'ly,* to and fro; I kissed my dear on ei-ther cheek, In the
bud of the morn-ing— O. A lark sang up from the
breez-y land, A lark sang down from a cloud a-far, As she and
I went hand in hand In the field where the dais-ies are.

*In Stephens' poem the word is "happily," which Barber chose to set on two notes rather than three.

The Windmill,
Rogers Park
July 20, 1927

CABIN

Tennessee Williams

Paul Bowles

SOMETIMES I FEEL LIKE A MOTHERLESS CHILD

African-American Spiritual
Arranged by Harry T. Burleigh

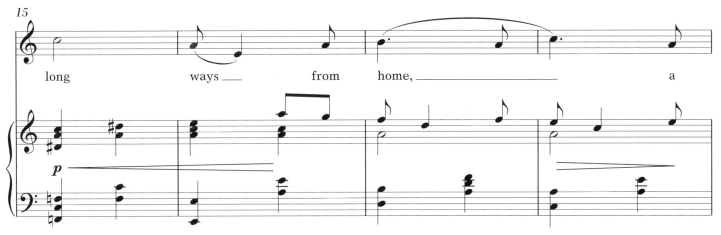

long   ways —— from   home, ——————————   a

p

rit.   *a tempo*

long   ways —— from   home. ————————   A

rit.   *a tempo*

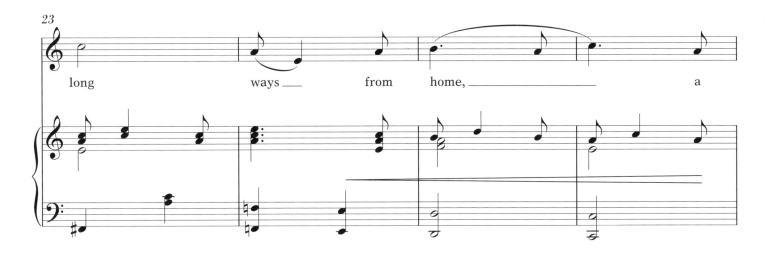

long   ways —— from   home, ————————   a

long   ways —— from   home. ————————

Some - times I

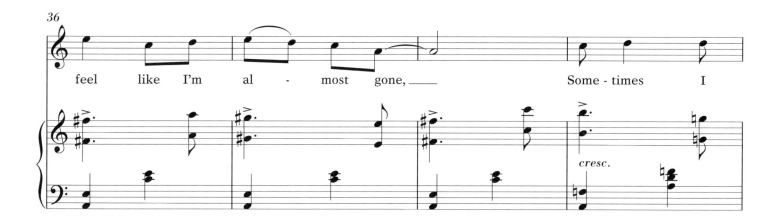

feel like I'm al - most gone, _____ Some - times I

feel like I'm al - most gone, _____ Some - times I

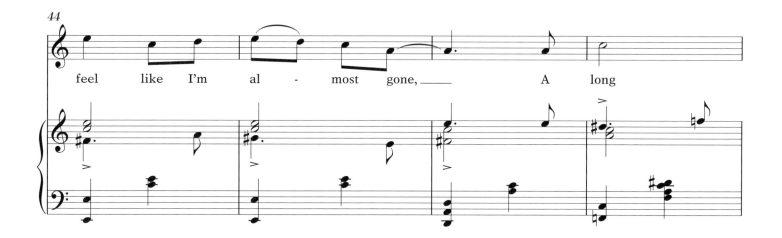

feel like I'm al - most gone, _____ A long

ways ___ from home, _____ a long ways __ from

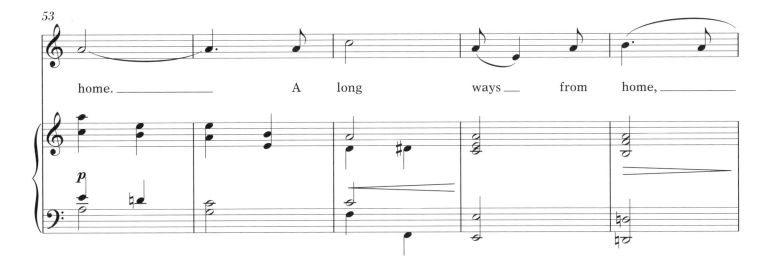

home. _____ A long ways __ from home, _____

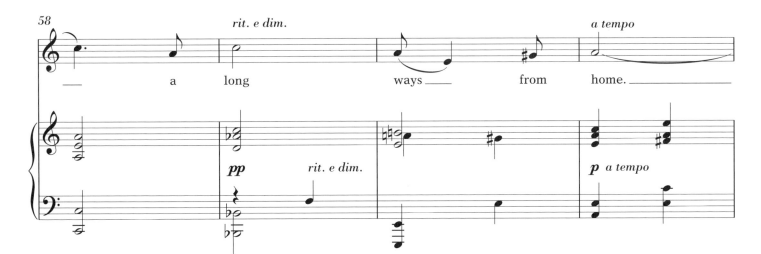

__ a long ways __ from home. _____

in memory of my brother, Ralph

ACROSS THE WESTERN OCEAN

Irish Sea Chanty
Arranged by Celius Dougherty

Oh, the times are hard and the wa - ges low, Oh, sai - lor, where you bound to? The Rock - y Moun - tains are my home, A - cross the west - ern

say good - bye, Oh, sai - lor, where you __ bound to?

Sis - ters, broth - ers, __ don't you __ cry, O'er the west - ern __

o - cean. Oh, the

times are hard and the wa - ges __ low, Oh, sai - lor, where you

COLORADO TRAIL

American Folksong
Arranged by Celius Dougherty

Sweet as the li-lac grows, Fair in the sun, Sal-ly was a pre-ty gal,

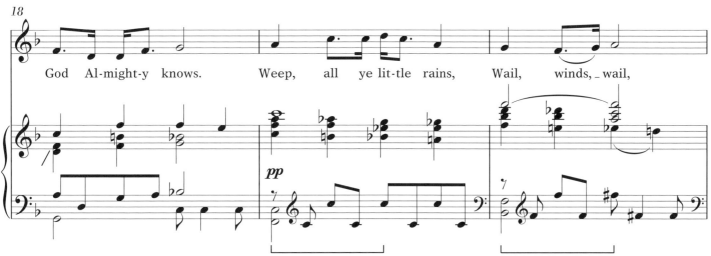

God Al-might-y knows. Weep, all ye lit-tle rains, Wail, winds, _ wail,

All a-long, a-long, a - long the Col - o-ra-do Trail. A-long the

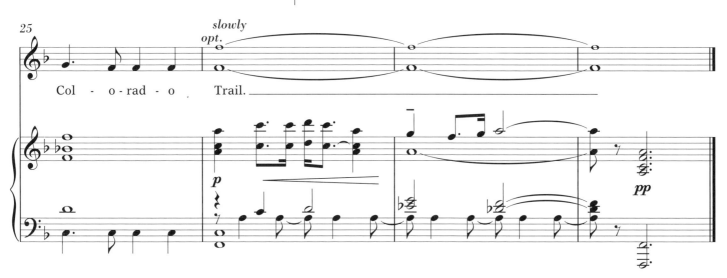

Col - o-rad - o Trail. _____

To Lawrence Tibbett

LOVELIEST OF TREES

A. E. Housman*

John Duke

* Poem from "A Shropshire Lad." Printed by permission of Grant Richards, London, publisher.

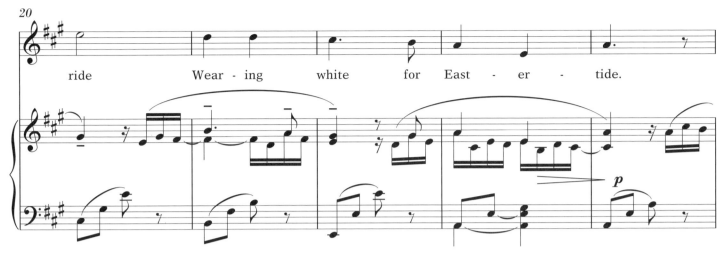

ride   Wear - ing   white   for   East - er - tide.

Now,   of   my   three - score   years   and   ten.

Twen - ty   will   not   come a - gain,   And

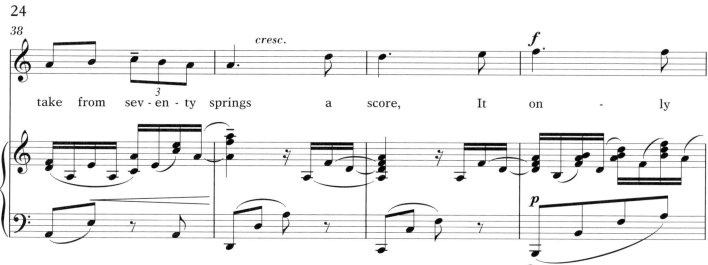

take from sev - en - ty springs a score, It on - ly

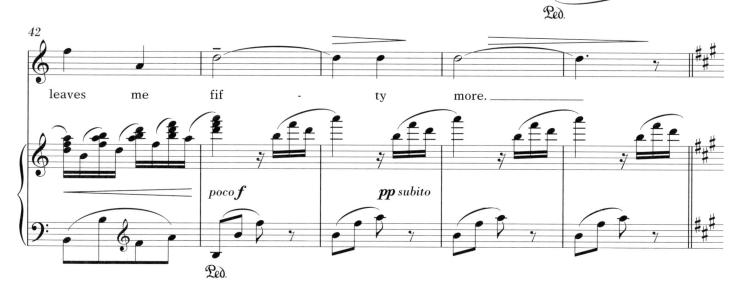

leaves me fif - ty more.

And since to look at things in bloom

Fif - ty springs are lit - tle room,

About the wood-lands I will go To

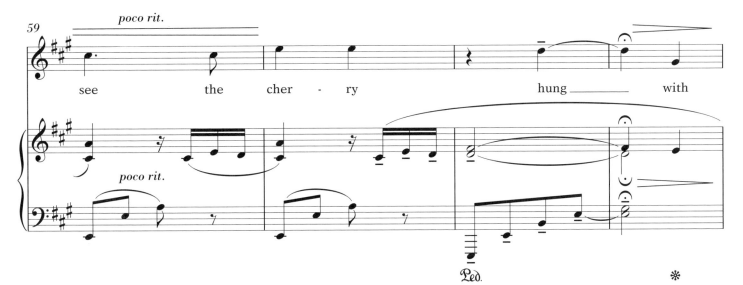

see the cher-ry hung with

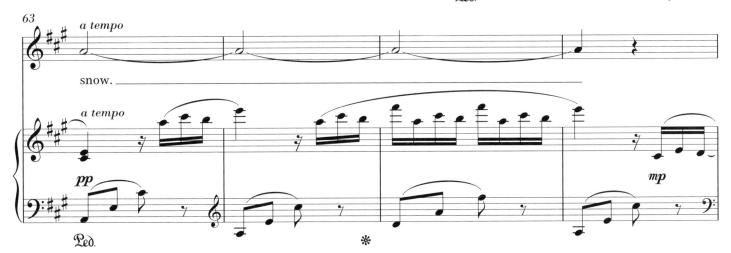

snow.

for Olive Endres

THE SHEPHERD

William Blake

Lee Hoiby

all the day _____ And his tongue shall be

filled _____ with praise. _____

For he hears _____ the lamb's in-no-cent call. ___

And __ he hears _____ the ewe's

ten - der _____ re - ply.   He is

watch - ful   when they are in peace,   For they   know   when their

shep - herd   is   nigh. _____

to the Guide
WHERE THE MUSIC COMES FROM

Words and Music by
Lee Hoiby

how. I want to sing to the ear - ly morn - ing, See the

sun - light melt the snow; And oh,____ I want to

grow.____

I want to

wake   to the liv-ing spir - it   Here in-side me where it lies.   I want to

lis - ten till I can hear   it,   Let it guide   me, and re - al - ize   That   I can

go   with the flow un - end - ing,   That is blend - ing,   that is

real;   And   oh, _____   I   want   to

feel.

I want to

walk in the earth-ly gar - den, Far from cit-ies, far from

fear. I want to talk to the grow-ing gar - den, To the

de - vas,* to the deer, And to be one with the riv - er flow - ing, Breez - es

blow - ing, sky a - bove;

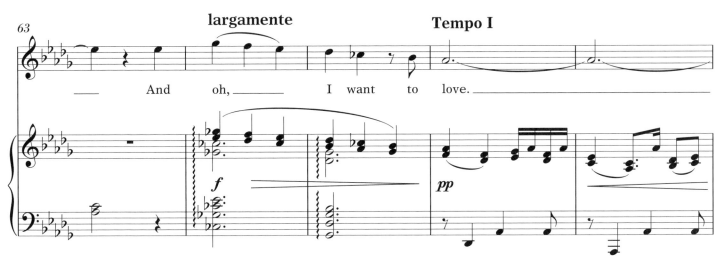

And oh, I want to love.

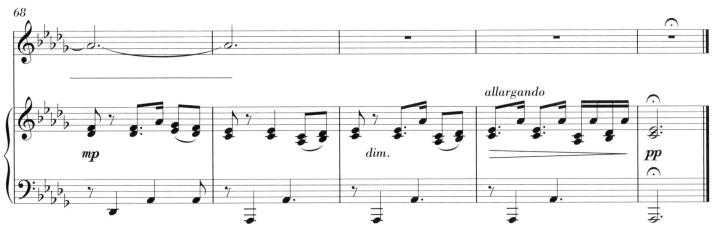

*pronounced *day – vas* (nature spirits)

BLACK IS THE COLOR
OF MY TRUE LOVE'S HAIR

Text collected and adapted by
John Jacob Niles
Music by John Jacob Niles

love _____ the grass where - on she stands.

I _____

love my __ love and __ well she knows, I love _____ the grass where -

on she goes; If __ she on __ earth no __ more __ I __ see, My

life _____ will quick-ly leave ___ me.

I _____ go to ___ Troub-le-some* to mourn, to weep, But

sat - is-fied I ne'er can sleep; I'll ___ write her a note in ___

a few lit-tle lines, I'll suf - fer death ten thou-sand times.

* Troublesome Creek, which empties into the Kentucky River.

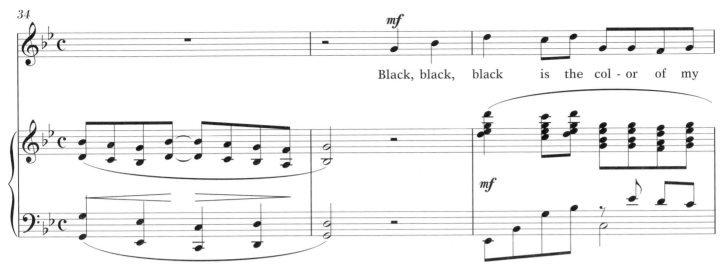

Black, black, black is the col - or of my

true love's hair, Her lips _____ are some-thing ro - sy fair, The _

pert - est _ face and the dain - ti - est _ hands– I love _____ the grass where-

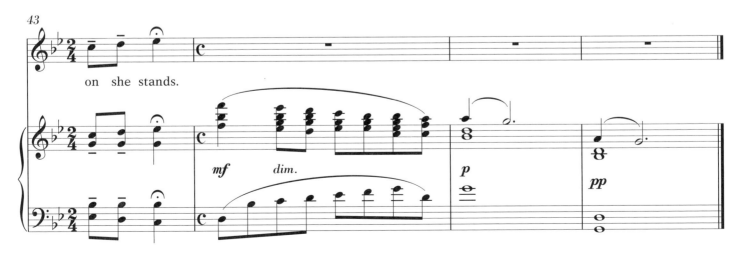

on she stands.

BROTHER WILL, BROTHER JOHN

Elizabeth Charles Welborn

John Sacco

ain't no use, Mis - ter, af - ter you're gone, ___ You

can't take it with you, Broth - er Will, Broth - er John.

You need - n't squeeze your coin tight in your hand, No

place for small change in the Prom - ised Land. It

ain't no use, Mis-ter, af-ter you're gone, __ You

can't take it with you, Broth-er Will, Broth-er John.

sly, provocative

Shake a leg here, shake a leg there,

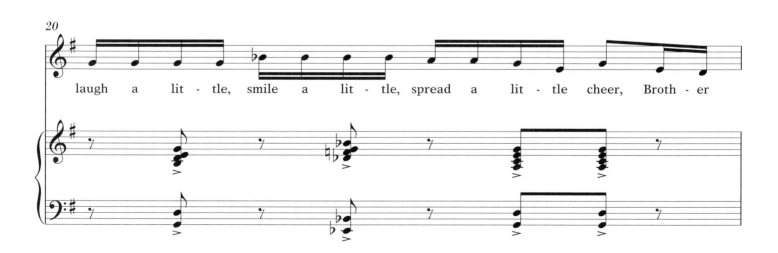

laugh a lit-tle, smile a lit-tle, spread a lit-tle cheer, Broth-er

Will, Broth - er John, Broth - er Will, Broth - er John, Broth - er

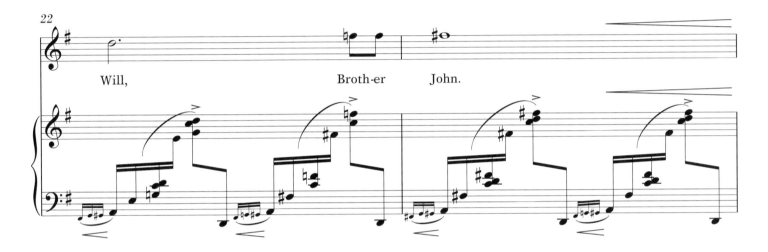

Will, Broth-er John.

Why mope a - round with fu - ne - re - al fac - es, Whip up your nag and

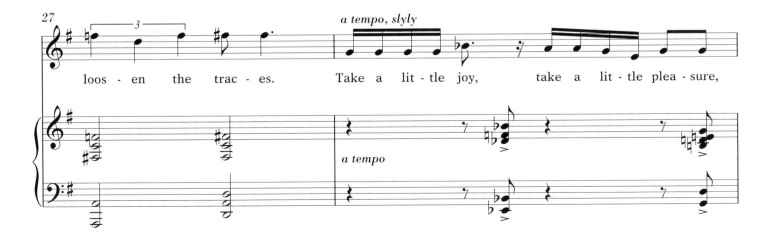

loos - en the trac - es. Take a lit - tle joy, take a lit - tle plea - sure,

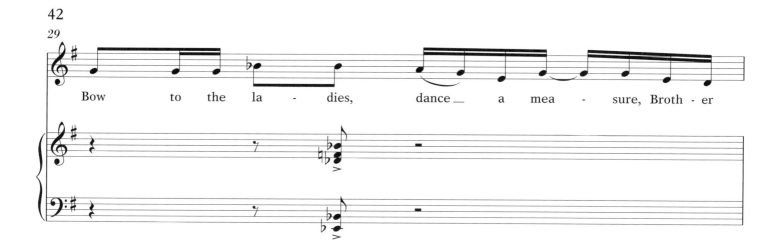

Bow to the la - dies, dance __ a mea - sure, Broth - er

Will, Broth - er John, Broth - er Will, Broth - er John, Broth - er

Will, Broth-er John.

You'll have to leave it when the cof - fin lid's on, ___ You

can't take it with you, Broth - er Will, Broth - er John, Broth - er

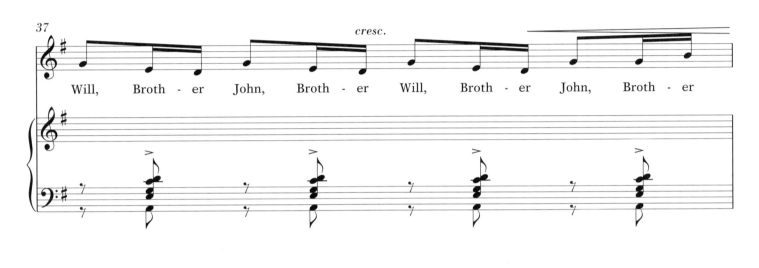

Will, Broth - er John, Broth - er Will, Broth - er John, Broth - er

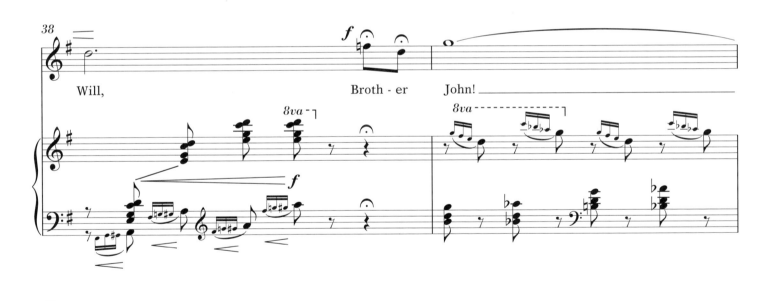

Will, Broth - er John!

ORPHEUS WITH HIS LUTE

William Shakespeare

William Schuman

show'rs There had made a last-ing spring. _____ Ev -'ry thing that heard him

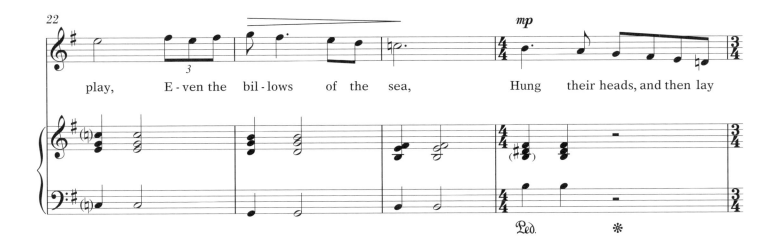

play, E - ven the bil - lows of the sea, Hung their heads, and then lay

by. _____ In sweet mu - sic is such art, Kill -ing care and grief of

heart, Fall a - sleep, or hear - ing, die. _____

THE SEA

from *8 Songs*

Edward MacDowell
Op. 47, No. 7

Broadly, with rhythmic swing

One sails_ a - way to_ sea, to_ sea, One stands on the shore_ and

cries;_____ The ship_ goes down the world, and_ the light_

On the sul - len wa - ter dies._____